Sex, Sperm, & STD'S

Sex, Sperm, & STD'S

What Every Teenage Boy Needs to Know

Rajasingam S. Jeyendran, Ph.D.
Megan Hollingsworth, B.S.

iUniverse, Inc.
New York Lincoln Shanghai

Sex, Sperm, & STD'S
What Every Teenage Boy Needs to Know

iUniverse books may be ordered through booksellers or by contacting:

iUniverse
2021 Pine Lake Road, Suite 100
Lincoln, NE 68512
www.iuniverse.com
1-800-Authors (1-800-288-4677)

Title page photograph,
by permission of CareNet Pregnancy Centers of Clallam County
(Copyright © 2001–2005, Hosted and Designed by BizMaxUSA)

ISBN-13: 978-0-595-37969-9 (pbk)
ISBN-13: 978-0-595-82338-3 (ebk)
ISBN-10: 0-595-37969-9 (pbk)
ISBN-10: 0-595-82338-6 (ebk)

Printed in the United States of America

For those men and boys who are curious yet confused, interested yet intimidated, and relaxed yet tense.

~R.S.J.

For those of you who have believed in me and shoved me in the water when I was too scared to jump right in.

~M.L.H.

Contents

Preface for the Boys

Weird things are happening to your body. You don't know what it is and you're not sure why it's there. This book will help you and your parents get through the roller coaster of life called *puberty*. You will learn about your own body, girls' bodies, sex, sexually transmitted diseases, sperm, infertility, and everything in-between. You and your parents can read this book cover to cover or simply use it as a reference; either way, it will be a useful tool through this strange and intense time in your life. After reading about sex, sperm, and STD's, you will better understand yourself and the world of reproduction.

Introduction

Our society has come a long way towards sexual freedom. Gender roles have slowly changed, and so have the issues of family, intimacy, and sexual expectations. Topics once considered wrong to talk about in polite, private conversation are now openly discussed in front of millions of viewers on TV and in the movies. All this information brings choices, however, and with these freedoms come important responsibilities. Many times, there are so many messages about sex in the media that they often just overwhelm teenagers instead of giving them practical advice about real-world issues and problems. Among all this open and straightforward conversation, sexuality itself is still a hotly debated and highly misunderstood subject. Today's teens live in a world of mixed signals and contradictory expectations. Many times, they are just confused and want answers to their questions about sex and developing.

When a teenager watches T.V., media images emphasizing violence, sex, and drugs try to represent what society wants to see. In reality, these images are unrealistic and unhealthy. Teens need to make good choices about expressing themselves sexually, and each teen has the power to do so. As children of the previous generation become parents of the new generation, shifting values show some of the natural conflicts between growing up and growing old. "Do as I say, and not as I did!" has become a saying for many a baby-boomer parents, trying hard to make up for the wildness of youth with the responsibilities of parenthood. While boys are forced to mature ever more rapidly into a society that seems even more confused than they are, these contradictions all add a new twist to the old saying, "Boys will be boys." Although independence and adventure seem essential to being a teenage male, <u>communication</u> and <u>guidance</u> are what most boys actually seek and what they so desperately need. Somewhere between mindless entertainment and formal education, teenage boys crave information about their sexual development and sexual experiences.

Sex is a natural part of human existence, yet few young men in our society understand their own sexuality, let alone its potential consequences. Various sexually transmitted diseases, including the continued threat of the virus causing AIDS, unwanted pregnancies, and the ongoing breakdown of family structures remind us that sexuality cannot be separated from consequence. For men struggling with fertility issues, a complete understanding of their own sexuality (from emotional aspects to the biological realities) is a good way to begin any treatment procedure. Understanding male sexual development and fertility is therefore as important a subject now as ever.

How should information about sex be communicated to teenage boys?

Sex education is as hot a topic as teen sex itself. How much information should adults give to children? How should we teach them, and toward what end? These all remain topics worthy of ongoing debate and analysis. Whether total abstinence or open-minded experimentation is "normal", most experts agree that true education and guidance must begin in the household. This book is best to read in a calm, open environment.

This text has been written as a complementary overview and reference work for young adult males and their parents. By reading and referencing this book, male teens and their parents will hopefully gain an interesting and informative resource to guide communication. With a bit of patience, commonly asked questions about male sexual development and fertility can be answered. The end-goal is maintenance of a calm, open, and relaxed environment where teenagers are able to have their many questions answered and their fears addressed. The importance of nurturing and keeping such an atmosphere cannot be over-emphasized; the first step toward mature, responsible adulthood is, after all, becoming a well-rounded teen.

To make this text easier to read, chapters are presented in a friendly and straightforward "Question & Answer" format. The authors hope this approach will simplify sometimes complicated and embarrassing subjects. Chapters can be read from beginning to end, skimmed for a general overview, or referenced to provide answers to specific questions. With attention and care, normal sexual response can be guided wisely and responsibly.

Male Sexual Development

Puberty: An Owner's Manual

At some point, every boy must physically and emotionally transform into a man. The differences between childhood and adulthood are certainly striking, and the whole transformation process can be life defining. This vital transitional period, known as "adolescence," or, more informally, as "puberty," can be a complex, difficult phase for boys and their families. Education and open communication are especially important as bodies and minds struggle among raging hormones and constantly changing social responsibilities.

So let's take a look at this wonderful and mysterious process. By doing so, hopefully some of the usual pain and confusion can be eased and perhaps avoided altogether.

Physical Changes

As if an identity crisis and concerns about the very meaning of life wouldn't be enough, every boy will sooner or later undergo intense and uncontrollable bodily changes. Although perfectly necessary and normal, to the teen these physical transformations might seem unique, strange, and scary. Since boys entering puberty are often somewhat emotionally confused, a firm understanding of these typical processes can make at least the biological foundation less surprising, and with some effort, less mysterious and frightening.

When is the right age for entering adolescence?

While the general characteristics of adolescence are common, when and to what extent they occur can vary a lot from boy-to-boy. Although nutrition can play a role, genetics seem the basic, unavoidable reason certain boys mature more or less rapidly than others. In other words, each child undergoes a series of complex changes over a period of time that can last several years and is determined by their own body. Consequently, boys and their parents don't need to "do" anything at all, but simply allow bodies and minds to adjust.

For boys, adolescence occurs between the ages of 10 and 18 years, and most often between 12 and 14 years of age. Again, the important thing is to allow the boy's own body to make these decisions for itself. Only if these changes seem highly unusual or abnormal should any attention be drawn to them, and a doctor eventually be consulted.

Are any of these changes common to both boys and girls?

Yes. The obvious differences between male and female puberty is that very different physical changes happen. However, some bodily changes are actually shared between the sexes, and include:

☑ **Height and Weight Increase**

Growth in all areas of the body is rapid during puberty, and an increase in height is typically the most notable. As body mass increases, the relative ratio of muscle and fat tissue greatly shift. These changes can lead to temporary bodily changes that might appear ugly or even abnormal. Although most teens can become alarmed at these changes, they are simply a natural way in which the human body adjusts itself during the obvious physical transformation from childhood to adulthood.

☑ **Hair, Skin and Voice**

Rapid growth in body hair in the armpits and in the genital areas is a normal part of puberty. Along with the growth of hair in these new areas, boys' voices get deeper and more "booming". Pimples and zits can appear on male and female teens' faces and bodies, although these skin blemishes are also a normal physical change.

What about the changes specific to just boys?

Identifying the specific physical transformations present as boys become men can help set a teenager's mind at ease. By reading through such a list and comparing these changes to the changes actually taking place in and on his own body, a teen can better accept them as normal, physical experiences.

Is it OK to talk about all this?

Yes, yes, YES! Openly discussing these changes, both with friends and family, can also relieve a lot of stress and possible confusion or shame. In fact, many if not most of the emotional problems that are troubling to teens have to do with fear and guilt. The "cure" usually involves openly communicating the easy answers to these otherwise tough questions.

Puberty Checklist For Boys

Physical Changes

☑ **Getting Taller and Bigger**

Outward and obvious signs include an increase in height. Such a growth spurt usually takes place between the ages of 12 and 14 years, but don't be concerned if you or your teen grows before or after this age range. Internal signs of such a rapid increase in height can involve so-called "growing pains," which include aches and pains in the bones and joints, particularly in the legs.

Muscles get larger as shoulders become broader. Hands and feet, and even the ears, also show definite growth. Due to the many rapid changes taking place throughout the teen's body, some of these growth spurts can appear unequal. The teen should be reassured, however, that with time, most of these apparent "irregularities" (overly large hands and ears, for instance) equal themselves out as the rest of the young man's body catches up.

Again, having an environment where such concerns can be calmly and safely addressed is very important. Teens need to know what is happening and why. Observing these changes in their own body and those of their peers, and then being able to inquire about them is important to every adolescent's self-esteem.

☑ The Genitals

Perhaps the most radical and potentially disorienting changes occur in the genital area. Pubic hair begins to grow dark and curly, starting where the penis joins the body. The hair expands outward, and eventually grows on the scrotum and around the anus. Sweat and oil glands also form and begin to produce fluids. The penis increases in size, and continues to grow throughout puberty. The scrotal sac darkens, becomes wrinkly, and begins to hang lower, accommodating growing testicles. The entire area increases greatly in sensitivity.

What's going on here? Should boys actually feel 'sexual'?

Without going into details of the emotional and behavioral changes common to puberty (those will be covered, in some detail, in later sections), most teenage boys suddenly find themselves with a robust, and seemingly uncontrollable, sex drive. Perhaps terrifyingly at first, teenage boys begin to experience erections randomly throughout the day and evening, in the form of nocturnal emissions, or so-called "wet dreams." For the first time, orgasm leads to the ejaculation of semen out of the penis. Masturbation becomes frequent, and ejaculation can and often does occur during sleep.

Although these physical changes and their additional behaviors can be an extremely embarrassing subject, especially among family, it is necessary to talk about them, at least in some form.

☑ **The Penis**

The human penis has two parts: The *shaft* and the *glans*, or head. The shaft is the cylindrical body, running from the base of the penis to its head. Along the underside of the shaft is the spongy body, which holds a thin tube, called the *urethra*. During urination, urine exits the penis through a small slit at the tip, which is called the *urinary opening*. Since the penis has only one opening and one such tube, semen is released along this same pathway.

Separating the shaft and glans is a ridge of skin around the lower part of the head, called the corona.

Is circumcision necessary? Why is it so routinely performed?

At birth, every male infant has a foreskin attached to the glans. The foreskin is an extension of skin at the head of the penis, and it can get infected or irritated when oily secretions, dead skin cells, dirt particles, sweat, and bacteria are allowed to gather underneath the foreskin, creating a sticky material called *smegma*. In most Western countries, including the United States, the surgical removal of the foreskin shortly after birth, in a process commonly called circumcision, prevents this condition. But improved hygiene and societal standards of cleanliness have perhaps made this procedure unnecessary. Others go even further and argue that removal of the foreskin decreases sensitivity and is potentially damaging. With the jury still out on the issue, the procedure is still done routinely, while some parents choose not to have it done on their baby boys.

Which sensation can arouse the most?

The penis has many nerves that make it sensitive to touch, pressure, and temperature. One particularly sensitive area is the corona, a ridge of skin around the lower part of the glans, or head, of the penis. For the most part, though, the human penis is most sensitive to friction. In contrast, the penises of other animals can be particularly responsive to heat, pressure, or other factors.

Size Matters Not

Peer pressure and the media have always held one major misconception: the bigger the penis, the better. This is not true; the size of your penis says absolutely nothing about your sexual abilities or fertility potential. In fact, the length of the penis is for the most part unimportant even during intercourse because the inner part of the vagina and cervix are not very sensitive.

Is there a match between the size and shape of penises and the animals who have them?

For the sake of curiosity and comparison, let's take a humorous look at the penises of other species. You might be surprised as to what is (and isn't!) out there. As you might suspect, the largest recorded average penis size in the animal kingdom is that of the whale. But don't start worrying over unfair comparisons; in fact, the penile size of an animal need not be proportionate to their overall mass at all. A great example is the gorilla. The gorilla's penis is typically only about an inch long when fully erect. Considering that gorillas can weigh over 400 pounds, you do the math!

Not only does penis size vary a lot from species to species, but the shape and structure of the penis changes, too. The penis of a pig, for example, actually takes on the shape of a corkscrew, perhaps explaining the basis for the term "screwing." Also, the penis of a dog contains a bone, which probably explains the phrase "boning" and reference to the erect penis itself as a "boner." Talking about house pets, cats actually have thorn-like structures on their penis. So, when you hear tomcats carrying on with their alley mates in the dead of night, all that high-pitched screaming seems reasonable. Not only are females penetrated with a prickly penis, but also tomcats bite their mates on the neck. If you think that's unfair and rough treatment, though, understand that such roughhousing has a biologically vital function: it actually makes the cat ovulate.

This Ain't No Bull!

Penises can be either stiff or soft. In the case of the bull, the penis is always rigid, and in an "S"-shape. When the bull is getting ready to mate, a muscle holding their penis in this folded shape relaxes, so the already rigid penis is extended into a more straight shape, down and out of the bull's body.

The Asian elephant, which has a soft penis, is also very odd. The female has a ventral vagina, which means that penetration can only be accomplished from below. Therefore, the elephant's penis must be very long, with only the last few inches curling up in order to enter the female from below. The African elephant, on the other hand, for unknown reasons has a stiff, straight penis. If you think this might be strange, the rhinoceros has a penis with flaps on the sides, and a head that looks like a blossoming flower.

Two-Timer

Whereas penis size can vary a lot from species to species, so can penis shape. One extreme example is the penis of some marsupials, which is actually bifurcated, or split into two! Such a bizarre shape evolved to accommodate the marsupial female, whose reproductive system has two lateral vaginas and a central pseudovaginal canal, usually closed until the approach of parturation. In other words, two vaginal canals, on either side of the birth canal, are used to transmit sperm into the female. During mating, the "split" penis is therefore actually able to enter and inseminating both vaginas simultaneously.

OK, enough with the wild safari. What about my own body?

Male Reproductive Anatomy

Biologically, everything the human body does is does for a reason: your immune system protects you from infection; your respiratory system provides you with energy from the oxygen you breathe; your circulatory system transports your blood to nourish the extremities of your body; and your reproductive system gives you the capacity to literally reproduce, or, more simply, have children.

What's the big deal about sex?

Unlike most of these biological systems, however, sexual reproduction, by definition, requires direct physical interaction with another human being. Sex therefore involves a very complicated network of interconnected and interdependent physiological, psychological, and sociologi-cal parts. Certain areas of sexuality are completely autonomous, or unconsciously controlled by your body, while others involve highly complex feedback systems between your brain, your reproductive organs, and your sexual interest in other human beings.

Where's a good place to start learning about sex?

A great place to start understanding male sexuality and fer-tility is the physical part of the equation, or the "how's" and "why's" of male biological reality. Learning this can help simplify an otherwise very complicated subject. By gaining a more thorough understanding of the body, or how and why it works the way it does, the male adolescent can better control and regulate its many functions, including the sexual ones. As the many changes occur which are characteristic of puberty, they can be understood as the natural and expected consequences of every boy becoming a man.

Great. But what about the emotional changes?

Once these physical transformations are better understood and even anticipated, their emotional consequences can be made much more enjoyable and less confusing. As the body changes, so does the mind; and as hormones begin to be produced and therefore influence, not only the body, but also a boy's behavior, every bit of information and communication helps.

Some History

One perhaps reassuring notion is that sex isn't only confusing to contemporary adolescents, but to many scientists and scholars throughout the ages. Before the beginning of modern technology and medical science, many even commonly asked questions about sexuality and reproduction were answered without much knowledge and only "guesses". Very gradually, and with much trial and error, these questions have been, for the most part, answered. Along the way, though, some fairly interesting and even humorous theories arose. Here are a few:

✝ One Early Idea

The ancient Greek philosopher Hippocrates theo-rized that semen was created in the brain and spinal column, and then secreted through the blood.

Obviously, medical science has come a long way since those early times, when the expression "having sex on the brain" was perhaps taken somewhat more literally.

✝ Aristotle Over Easy

Another Greek who influenced scientific thinking from ancient times all the way through the Middle Ages, Aristotle, theorized that the human female had nothing at all to do with reproduction, aside from being a mere "holding tank". He reached such a sur-prising conclusion based on practical evidence: since a man's semen could be seen, while the female's egg, unlike a chicken's, remained invisible, the human egg was therefore non-existent. This theory really doesn't live up to the saying, "It takes two to tango."

Contemporary Concepts

Although science has admittedly come a long way since the days of sperm brains and motherless human babies, we still have much to learn. Thankfully, contemporary science is able to provide a fairly thorough understanding of male reproductive physiology, and the relationship between form and function.

Missions: Possible

The male reproductive system was designed by nature to do essentially two things.

① **Mission One**

   Create a "male genetic information" carrier. We call this tiny capsule containing the biological blueprint "sperm".

② **Mission Two**

   Deliver these carrier cells to the potential fertilization site, inside a woman's body where contact can be made with her "egg".

English, please!

The concept is much simpler than it might at first seem. Essentially, the male reproductive system has been designed to create sperm, and deliver it to the egg within the female. As such, the different parts of the male reproductive system (some visible as organs outside the body, others deep within) assist either aspect of this process. As you read and learn about male physiology, keep in mind that these organs either help create or deliver sperm.

There's gotta be more to it than that, right?

Although conceptually this process sounds rather straightforward, the actual course of action is extremely complicated, and involves many diverse, interconnected physiological, chemical, biomechanical and even psychological elements. But for now, let's stick with the basics.

Two Organs

Form and function are intertwined from the ground up. Not surprisingly, then, the two anatomically obvious parts of the male reproductive system are the actual sperm *creation* and *delivery* organs:

① **Sperm Creation Factory: The Scrotum**

The scrotum is that hanging sack of skin beneath the penis, housing the testicles, or testes, which are the biological factories actually creating sperm.

② **Sperm Delivery Mechanism: The Penis**

The penis functions as the primary sperm delivery organ. When sexually stimulated, the penis becomes rigid and capable of penetrating the female body and then releases sperm in very large quantities.

Male genetic information carried by the sperm is thereby brought directly to female genetic information carried by the egg, which is inside the female reproductive system at the fertilization site.

The Sperm Factory

Anatomically, the two testes inside the scrotum are about equal in size (2 x 3/4 x 1 1/4 inches). Each testicle holds long, ultra-small tubules, which are closely wrapped together, and if stretched out, would run for miles. Inside the walls of these tiny tubes, germ cells (called "spermatogonia") grow by the millions and millions. They divide and mature through a series of complex biological processes ("spermatogenesis"), eventually separating from the tubular surface and developing into mature sperm (see Figure 1). These so-called spermatogonia constantly replace themselves during this cell division process, which explains why a man can continually produce healthy sperm well into old age.

How many sperm does a man create, and how often?

The entire spermatogenetic process, involving cell creation, division and maturation from original germ cell to fertile sperm cell, requires about 70 days. On average, a male will create over 50 million sperm cells every single day of his life, constantly repeating this little-over-two-month cycle from spermatogonian to mature sperm cell.

Interestingly enough, this 70-day-cycle can help explain why men sometimes experience semen quality problems over two months after having a fever or sustaining an injury.

Figure 1: Representation of the human spermatozoon

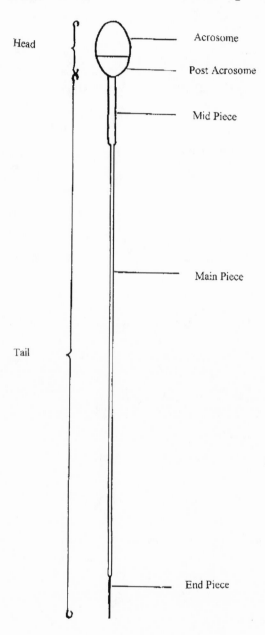

What's the relationship between temperature and sperm creation and health?

Actually, the relationship between temperature and sperm creation is pretty basic.

•• Too Hot To Handle

> For biochemical reasons of their own, sperm are extremely picky about their environment. Sperm must be created and stored where the average temperature remains at least four degrees *lower* than standard body temperature. Such a need to stay cooler than your average body heat explains why the testes hang in a sack *outside* the body. If testes were internal, like the female ovaries, the environment would simply be too hot for sperm to be properly created and stored for any significant length of time.

That loose bag of skin lying beneath the penis is technically called the *scrotum*, or scrotal sac. In fact, as a result of sexual stimulation, exercise, or exposure to cold, the layer of muscle fibers connecting the sac to the body contract and loosen on their own, creating a kind of natural thermostat for the maintenance of temperature control. In hot weather, for example, the connecting muscles loosen, causing the scrotum to move more freely, moving the heat around better. When the scrotum moves closer to the body in cold weather, in contrast, it is trying to conserve heat by keeping the testes closer to the body.

You may have, at some time or other, referred to these organs as "balls." The word "testis," by the way, comes from the Latin word for "witness." The words "testify" and "testament" came from the same root. The Romans would make an oath to tell the truth by holding their testicles — perhaps equating the essence of manhood with honesty, or, as some historians have observed, implying that lying under oath could lead to castration! "I swear to tell the truth, the whole truth, and nothing but the truth..." Under such conditions, wouldn't you?

Can heat affect fertility then?

Yes (but often times no). Sperm are so choosy, in fact, that any increase in overall body temperature caused by, say, working in a very hot environment or having a high fever, will interfere or even destroy sperm production and maintenance. Men suffering from a high fever, as already mentioned, will experience a marked drop in sperm count and quality roughly two months after their high temperature breaks, since spermatogenesis takes about that long to create new sperm cells.

Thankfully, though, spermatogenesis is a hard-working process: If no permanent damage occurred to the testes, the process can resume when body conditions normalize; healthy sperm will be available for reproduction about 70 days after that recovery date. Similarly, relatively short exposure to extreme temperatures (such as relaxing in a sauna or whirlpool) has little effect on fertility and sperm production. And remember that apparent myth about tight underwear and sterility? Well, don't be too concerned, unless, of course, you're tackling a fertility issue; in that case, think about wearing those boxers. If fertility issues become important later in life, however, exposure to temperature extremes should be considered as one of many possible causes.

Are other species also affected in this way?

Yes. Interestingly enough, the fertility of cattle goes significantly down during the hot summer months, for this very same reason.

What does a sperm look like, and why?

♦ Tiny Tadpoles

The spermatozoa (usually called, simply for convenience sake, "sperm") is a tiny cell of about 1/500th of an inch long and consists of a *head* and *tail* (see figure

2). The head is oval in shape, tapering towards the tip, just like a spearhead.

As you probably know, sperm are designed to move. Not only move, but once close to the egg, puncture it and deliver genetic material inside the egg.

In practice, the sperm tail moves back and forth, pushing the entire structure along through whatever media happens to be present. Obviously, this movement plays a vital role for sperm movement through the female reproductive system following sexual intercourse.

Figure 2: Electron Micrograph of Human Spermatozoa

Sperm Facts

The sperm nucleus makes up approximately 65 percent of the head and consists of genetic material (mostly DNA, or so-called "deoxyribonucleic acid," the molecule that contains the male genetic coding sequence). The back portion of the head is covered by a sac-like structure that contains enzymes which act something like a biochemical warhead, helping the sperm to penetrate the surface of the egg if direct contact is made.

The tail is about 10 times the length of the head. The strongest part of the tail produces the energy needed for sperm movement, which results from back-and-forth movements of the tail itself. In other words, a man's sperm look and swim like tiny tadpoles, shaking their tales back and forth to blindly push themselves forward, trying to reach and fertilize that female egg that is deep inside the female reproductive system.

In this sense, sperm are more like torpedoes because they are able to move forward and penetrate without the help of anything else.

What about the sperm of other species?

☑ The Sperm Germ

Just as penis length and even structure can vary greatly from species-to-species, so, too, can their sperm.

To cite some examples, consider the sperm of the honey possum. Although the animal is a small marsupial, its sperm is more than eight times the length of human sperm, and the tip is shaped like a sharp spearhead. The head of rodent sperm is actually hooked, while a koala bear's sperm head is like a pointy corkscrew. So, small animals might have large sperm, and vice versa.

Sperm structure for different species depends on how it fertilizes their eggs. Reptilian and avian sperm seem to have no noticeable head. These sperm look like long, thin tubes, with the upper end only slightly thicker than the tail. One interesting feature of these sperm is their ability to survive for days within the female. For example, turkeys and hens can lay fertilized eggs for many days after a single mating. In the case of fish, sperm tend to be rounder, with a short tail. Since fertilization occurs outside the female's body, these fish sperm remain active for only a very short period of time (only a few seconds!). As an extreme example, bat semen is very toxic, and is capable of lying still within the female bat for *months*.

In summary, sperm size and shape, just like to the dimensions of animal penises, evolved in a very specific manner to improve fertilization opportunities. In other words, male parts are designed to fit best with their female complements, namely, the female reproductive system and the oocyte, or egg. Just as the penis is designed to best penetrate the vagina, so, too, are sperm designed to best fertilize the egg.

Human sperm is weird enough. Tell me more.

Aside from the obvious difference between the female egg and the male sperm, it is interesting to note that there are some important differences between them. Why is it that one egg passively waits in the Fallopian tubes, while hundreds of sperm must aggressively try to reach it?

What evolutionary significance can this complex process have?

For most species in the wild, females mate with numerous males during the course of any given reproductive cycle. Consequently, sperm from many different males must "fight it out" to be the one special sperm that actually reaches the egg and fertilizes it.

Is there a variation in sperm production between species?

Producing the most sperm possible is obviously an advantage over others. Given the difference in reproductive dynamics and physiology, of course, many differences exist in sperm production rates between different species. For example, consider:

SPECIES DIFFERENCES IN VOLUME AND SPERM COUNT OF EJACULATED SEMEN

SPECIES	VOLUME (ML)	AVERAGE SPERM COUNT (MILLION/ML)
Boar	250	100
Bull	6	1,000
Dog	9	300
Goat	1	3,000
Man	3	80

Rabbit	1	150
Ram	1	3,000
Stallion	70	120
Turkey	0.3	7,000

Sperm production is very much tied to the mating habits of species. The presence of a sperm "container" in the female human makes excessive sperm production unnecessary, since sperm can fertilize her egg many hours, or even days, after intercourse.

Okay, but what about me? How many sperm does a human usually produce?

☑ **Quantity over Quality**

On average, a man produces about 50 million sperm a day (or about 500 sperm per second!). Of these, very little is needed for actual fertilization to work. Given the tremendous volume of production, workmanship can get sloppy, even with the best of biological quality controls.

Ultimately, "quantity over quality" is the male reproductive motto, virtually the opposite saying of the female system, which typically creates, protects and relies on only a *single* reproductive cell per month.

Okay. But what exactly happens between the Sperm Factory and Delivery?

Sperm Express

Sperm are created in the testes in the scrotum, are stored, and then transported through the male reproductive system, and are finally released from the penis.

Perhaps the best way to understand the entire journey is to describe the various stages, or "stations" along the complicated route. Remember that each "stop" has a particular function. If each "stop" didn't have its own function, the sperm would not be ready to begin its journey into the female reproductive system. See figure 3 on page 33 for a diagram of the entire process.

1. *Testes (to epididymis)*: Sperm are created here from starter cells via the spermatogenetic process. When sperm are mature enough, they move out of the testes and enter the *epididymis* (e-pi-Di-di-mis), a single, highly complicated glandular "tube" that, if unwound, would be more than six meters in length.

2. *Epididymis (to vas deferens)*: Anatomically, the epididymis is divided into head, body and tail parts. Sperm travel from the testes into the attached epididymal head, and then work their way through the epididymal body, where many different chemical and morphological changes happen to the sperm. Epididymal fluids are also added to the sperm,

creating the beginning of seminal fluid. Sperm travel slowly through the epididymis, and are stored in the epididymal tail until they are ejaculated. The enhanced sperm, safely contained and now nourished in fluid, quickly exit through the epididymal tail during ejaculation.

3. *Vas deferens (vas DE-fer-ins) (to accessory sex glands):* The epididymal tail leads directly into the *vas deferens*, another glandular tube, this one approximately 15 inches long in total length. During ejaculation, the sperm cells and fluid stored in the epididymis are suddenly carried into the vas deferens, where additional seminal components are added to the mix from the *accessory sex glands* (see next section). When men choose to get a vasectomy, this is the area that is surgically cut.

4. *Urethra (YOO-reeth-ruh) (and out of penis)*: The vas deferens joins with the urethra, a tube shared with the bladder. A valve closes off the bladder during ejaculation to prevent semen from entering the bladder, and also to prevent urine from getting into the semen. The urethra runs all the way through the penis, ending at the open tip, where both urine and semen can each leave the body (separately).

5. *Penis (PEE-niss)*: The sperm end their journey through the male reproductive system through this organ which, when sexually stimulated, becomes erect. The penis is then able to penetrate into the female reproductive system, where sperm can be deposited deep inside the vagina.

To make a long story short, these organs nourish and provide important ingredients to the semen. This liquid is a thick, strong blend of fluids that can protect, nourish and carry the sperm until they can enter the female reproductive system.

The so-called "accessory sex glands" are several glands that add many complex and extremely important biochemicals to the sperm as they enter the vas deferens.

Figure 3: The Male Reproductive System

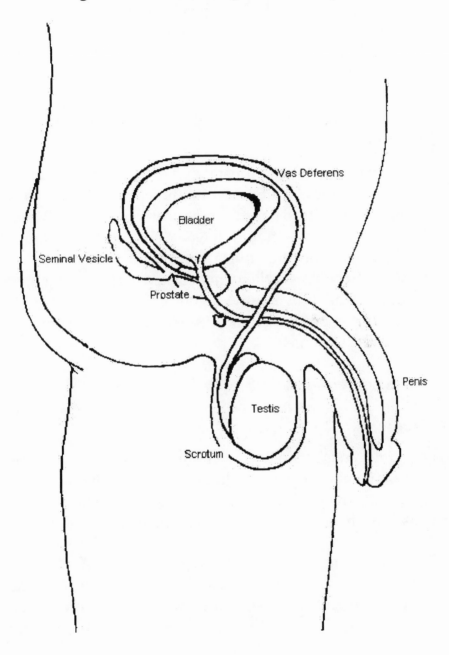

These glands are made up of the *seminal vesicles*, the *ampulla* of the vas deferens, the *prostate gland*, and the *Cowper's (bulbourethral) gland*. Each gland creates various parts that, when added all up (combined with the sperm, of course), form the *semen (SEE-men)*.

Is that one gland the same "prostrate" that can be a cancer risk?

Yes. Of these glands, the prostate, as a result of its location and unique glandular architecture, is most prone to infection and cancer. Physicians highly recommend that all men over the age of 40 should have their prostrate glands checked at least once or twice a year, since it is easier to cure health problems if they are detected early. Young men should keep this preventative outlook in mind, since studies suggest that prostrate cancer is one of the most common forms of cancer in men.

What is semen made of?

Ingredients

The *seminal vesicles* alone contribute approximately 75 percent to overall ejaculate volume. The prostate provides another 20 percent; all other secretions plus the sperm cells themselves make up the remaining 5 percent.

The fluids from these glands are collectively called the *seminal plasma* of the ejaculate. This seminal plasma provides sperm nourishment, protection from "bad germs", and transportation. The plasma also contains anti-bacterial and immune suppressive factors, which fight off infection and disease.

Even more importantly, semen helps protect the sperm as they enter the female reproductive system, which can contain sperm-killing cells in the vaginal mucous. The ingredients in the semen allow as many sperm as possible to actually make it to the egg, or *oocyte*.

Swimming Upstream

Of the millions upon millions of spermatozoa ejaculated into the vagina during a standard male ejaculation, less than one percent actually reaches the uterus. Of these, only one to five thousand spermatozoa are actually able to make it to the fertilization site. One sperm may or may not successfully fertilize the egg, which simply depends on chance and luck.

All excess spermatozoa die and disintegrate, or are more actively removed from the female reproductive system by white blood cells. Some actually leave the tract by passing into the abdominal cavity.

No Hurry

Interestingly enough, a few spermatozoa reach the fertilization site within minutes following insemination; many sperm actually penetrate into the inner female tract a few hours after sex.

The so-called "sperm reservoir" effect can help heighten the chance of fertilization, since a woman's window of fertility is typically very narrow. By pooling the sperm at the base of the cervix, sperm-egg contact can be extended over many days. In other words, actual conception can occur as much as a week after sex.

For this reason, human semen doesn't need to hold as many sperm as the semen of other animals. In other words, most animals must fertilize their mates during or immediately following mating; human beings, on the other hand, are capable of pooling their semen in "containers" within the female reproductive system. Fertilization can therefore occur hours, or even days after, actually having sex.

Limited Capacity

Sperm cells, even though fully mature, cannot fertilize an egg until certain membrane changes (called "capacitation") take place on the sperm cell surface, which is triggered by the female reproductive tract itself.

In other words, a man may produce *potentially* fertile sperm, but his partner's body actually decides if his sperm is fully fertile upon contact with various biochemicals within her own reproductive system. Significantly, once the egg is actually fertilized, chemicals are released to both stop this "detective" reaction, and to seal off the egg's boundary layers, preventing any additional sperm from penetrating the egg.

In a sense, it's definitely "winner take all" when it comes to sperm and fertilization. Some may say it's "every sperm for himself". As an interesting consequence, all in vitro (test tube) fertilization procedures must artificially induce this same "detective" reaction for fertilization to successfully take place.

Can a man actually produce "female sperm"?

Female Sperm

Sort of. Most people, if asked, would conclude that all sperm cells are, by definition, male (in the sense that they contain exclusively male genetic material). After all, the female oocyte, or egg, contains exclusively female genetic material, so what would be the sense or practical point of having a *female* sperm cell?

Given a bit of consideration, however, and knowing that, since female eggs are exclusively "female" in their genes (being female is therefore the official "default sex" for all human beings), the truth becomes obvious.

World Without Women

A man has 23 pairs (46 total) of chromosomes in every cell, plus two so-called sex chromomes, which for men are both an "X" and a "Y". A woman, on the other hand, has those 23 pairs (also 46 total), plus two "X"s. In other words, what makes a boy different from a girl is basically this one extra sex chromosome; if it's an "X", then the person is a woman (46XX), and if the extra chromosome is a "Y", the person is a man (46XY).

During spermatogenesis (sperm creation in the testes), the 46 total chromosomes split into two: One sperm with 23 chromosomes and an "X", and the other sperm with 23 chromomes and a "Y". Similarly, during oogenesis (egg creation in the ovaries), the 46 chromosomes break into two, both of which contain 23 chromomes and an "X". (Only one of these chromosome groups will potentially grow into the egg.)

When the sperm fertilizes the egg, each cell therefore contributes 23 chromosomes plus one sex chromosome, for a total of 46 chromosomes and two sex chromosomes, to make a complete set. Since each egg automatically will contribute an "X" chromosome, and sperm can deliver either an "X" or a "Y", the resulting gender of the offspring depends entirely on the sperm. In other words, the man's sperm determines whether the child will be a boy or a girl!

In slightly more technical terms, then, if a "female sperm" with its X chromosome fertilizes the egg, then the resulting child will be a girl (23X + 23X = 46XX). If a "male sperm" with its distinctive Y chromosome fertilizes the egg, then the resulting child will be a boy (23X + 23Y = 46 XY). See figure 4 for a visual explanation.

Figure 4: Gender Schematics

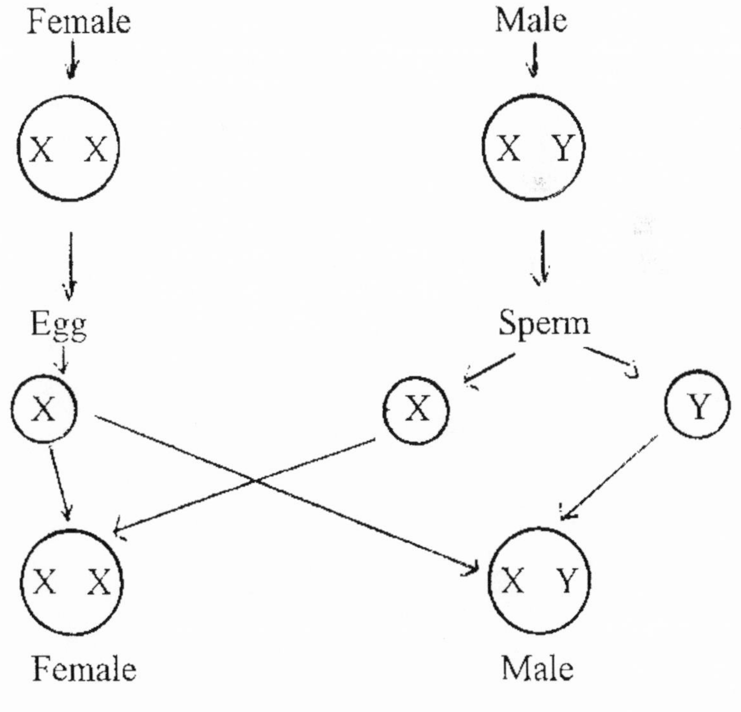

Female   Male

(X X)   (X Y)

Egg   Sperm

(X)   (X)   (Y)

(X X)   (X Y)

Female   Male

Male Sexual Response

Sexual behavior cannot be separated from the biological functions of reproduction. Focusing on the physical stages of *sexual arousal* can thereby help simplify an otherwise complicated and confusing biological reality. Too often, feelings of shame, guilt, and uncertainty override a natural and healthy instinct. Learning about male sexual response in an open, honest manner can help correct these negative feelings, and sufficiently prepare teenagers for a responsible and rewarding adulthood.

How is sexual stimulation different from other types of nervous response?

Sexual stimulation is, from a neurological viewpoint, no different from any other sensation. Nerves are stimulated in a particular part of the body, and signals from these areas travel to the brain as electrical impulses. The brain then analyzes and interprets these signals, triggering a complex system of reflexes involving the sex organs and the brain on many different physical and mental levels.

The favored form of sexual response varies between individuals: Some men are more visually aroused, while others may naturally prefer verbal or physical contact. Regardless of the preferred form of stimulation, however, sex begins and ends in the brain. The brain has conscious and unconscious elements, so sexual arousal can be either voluntary or involuntary.

Okay, what actually happens to me when I get sexually excited?

Sexual Response Cycle

From a biological viewpoint, the physical process of sexual arousal and release typically follows a basic pattern. Understanding this pattern can help teens understand and better control this so-called sexual response cycle. And as boys become men, awareness and sensitivity to this cycle can enhance the pleasure and intimacy of sexual relationships in adulthood.

The sexual response cycle can be broken down into four basic stages: *excitement, plateau, orgasm, and resolution.* Remember, however, that the exact timing and specific dynamics of each stage can vary not only between individuals, but also from one sex act to another.

Stage 1: Excitement

Physical signs of sexual arousal begin with a noticeable increase in heart and breathing rate, and a slight rise in body temperature. The skin flushes, cheeks redden, and muscles throughout the body can tighten.

Once sexual stimulation begins, an erection can occur within seconds. Essentially, the "aroused" brain causes the expansion of important arteries, which, in turn, shrink certain veins. Spongy tissues of the penis fill with blood, which stiffen the entire organ and do not allow the blood to escape, which "traps" the blood inside the penis and keeps the erection. Contrary to popular belief, this blood flow cycle is the sole means to an erection, no muscle or bone movement causes the penis to become erect. Only the dog has a bone in its penis. During this first phase, the scrotum tightens, and the testes rotate and move closer to the body. Within the brain, chemicals called *endorphins* are released, which greatly heighten the feeling of pleasure. Interestingly enough, these brain chemicals allow men to feel opposite sensations at the same time: They become tense, yet more relaxed; the mind feels highly focused yet free of any anxiety.

During this initial excitement phase, the sex glands begin to secrete. These secretions slowly build, increasing the internal pressure of the male reproductive system (and, indirectly, the overall sexual pleasure). Allowing this first phase more time can actually heighten the degree of sexual pleasure, and even result in a more powerful and satisfying orgasm. Learning how to control this phase can also become an important part of any teen's development, and result in heightened sexual pleasure later in life. Paying more attention to the excitement phase can help achieve greater sensitivity and intimacy when the male is with a sexual partner. With his own sexual dynamic better in check, a man can better focus on the needs and pleasures of his partner.

Stage 2: Plateau Phase

Sexual arousal that begins in the excitement phase is maintained and strengthened during the *plateau phase*. Essentially, the plateau phase is the body's way of preparing for the upcoming orgasm. As with the other phases, plateau can vary greatly in intensity and time between individuals, and from one sexual cycle to the next in the same person. In general, men who have trouble controlling ejaculation have a very brief plateau stage.

All arousal characteristics of the excitement phase increase as the body enters the plateau phase. Heart rate and body temperature both increase further, as muscles throughout the body flex and tighten in anticipation of orgasm. The penis becomes flushed and completely filled with blood, often leading to a darkening in the penis head and scrotum. The testicles rise even closer to the body. The teen might also notice drops of seminal fluid (originating from the Cowper's gland) "leaking" from the penis at this point, in anticipation of total orgasmic release, or *ejaculation*.

What does this plateau phase have to do with sexual control?

As boys mature physically and emotionally, their capacity to control the plateau phase increases tremendously. At first, the transition from excitement to orgasm might seem quick and unavoidable. With some "practice," however, teens can learn to control the plateau phase, and thereby better control their entire sexual dynamic.

Stage 3: The "Big O"

Orgasm is the peak of the sexual response cycle. As the body moves from plateau to orgasm, a "point of no return" has been reached, leading to what's sometimes called "ejaculatory inevitability". Since orgasm is what leads to the release of sperm from the male's body, orgasm can be understood as the end-goal of the male sexual and reproductive function.

Orgasm is physiologically the most complex of the phases, and proceeds through a fixed sequence of events inside the body.

First, an orgasm is characterized by a surge of energy, which seems to erupt throughout the body. The technical term for such muscular excitation and release is *myotonia*. Some describe the exciting sensation as electricity flowing suddenly throughout the back, arms, legs, and genitals. The face flushes and can make extreme expressions. The brain seems to "explode" in a sudden and intense flurry of ecstatic activity. At the same time that these wonderful sensations are happening, involuntary contractions in the prostrate, vas deferens and seminal vesicles send semen into the base of the urethra, ready for expulsion from the penis. Within a few seconds of this initial surge of energy, highly charged (and highly pleasurable) muscle contractions in the male reproductive tract and along the length of the penis rapidly lead to "ejaculation." This is, by definition, the energetic release of semen from the penis, usually in three to five spurts. Because the semen must travel through the urethra for a period of time, the semen is not outwardly visible until shortly after ejaculatory inevitability is reached. The fluids released during ejaculation also follow a fixed sequence: first, a small amount of Cowper's gland fluid is extruded; next, the prostatic fluid and the spermatozoa (about 0.5 ml); and finally, the secretions of the seminal vesicles (about 1.0–3.0 ml). Overall, though, the total volume of semen released during a typical ejaculation is about 2.5ml, or roughly a half a teaspoon.

What is "retrograde ejaculation," and how does it occur?

During ejaculation, the urinary tract to the bladder closes, which is necessary in order to prevent semen from flowing back into the bladder. If the neck of the urinary bladder does not close off, semen spurts into the bladder, leading to so-called "retrograde ejaculation." Men who have undergone prostate surgery or suffer from multiple sclerosis or diabetes may have this problem. One unfortunate effect of retrograde ejaculation is that it renders the man infertile. Boys may also suffer from retrograde ejaculation for behavioral reasons. The condition may occur when the boy for one reason or another doesn't want to ejaculate while masturbating. To avoid ejaculation, the boy may put his finger over the tip of his penis, blocking the flow of semen. Although this will initially stop the release, it may also lead to subsequent pain and discharge from the penis. Boys should know that such behavior is unnatural and unhealthy, and can lead to severe physical problems if unchecked. Although ejaculation without an orgasm is possible, for the healthy male, ejaculation and orgasm are naturally intertwined. On the other hand, boys who have not yet reached puberty commonly have orgasms without ejaculation. In fact, one of the first objective signs that puberty has been conclusively reached is when a boy notices ejaculation following orgasm.

Stage 4: Resolution

The *resolution phase* follows immediately after orgasm. Unlike women who can orgasm repeatedly during arousal, men must repeat the entire sexual response cycle after achieving orgasm. After ejaculation the male must spend some time "recuperating". During this refractory period, both orgasm and ejaculation are physically impossible.

The most obvious sign that the resolution phase has begun is that the erection ends. Known as *detumescence*, the veins of the penis dilate during orgasmic contractions, causing the penis to become limp. Without further sexual stimulation, the testes will also slowly lower into the scrotum. The entire body will relax and slowly return to its normal, unaroused state. If orgasm is not reached during a particular cycle, resolution will usually take longer. The street slang for this term is "blue balls," which is sometimes given as an excuse to continue sexual activity. Although there may be some slight discomfort, there is no physical pain involved in not reaching an orgasm during the sexual cycle.

Emotional Changes

Adolescence can be the most difficult period of a person's life. Although the physical changes normally characteristic of puberty can seem extreme, the emotional transformation from boy to man is perhaps the greatest challenge.

Self-esteem can be a problem for most adults, let alone for teenagers studying themselves in the mirror. Radical changes in height and weight, hair in new places, and blemishes all add to the confusion and emotional trauma.

We live in a culture that puts tremendous emphasis on material things. Peer pressure, reinforced by media images, strongly and repeatedly suggest to teens that human worth is based on fancy possessions and perfect bodies. Since wealth isn't really something a teen can control, potentially destructive and unrealistic emphasis on physical perfection is often stressed. Unfortunately, adolescence is the one time in life when the human body is rapidly and often unevenly changing; skin blemishes and a host of other bodily imperfections are a natural and inevitable part of growing up. Consequently, boys should be made aware not only that these physical changes are normal, but that the most important part of growing up is learning how to differentiate what's on the surface from what's inside and actually important.

These changes going on inside, of course, can be even more confusing and intense than the physical changes of puberty. To help clarify and share some of these, the most common emotional changes boys experience during puberty include:

☺☹ **Moodiness**

Sudden and unexpected mood shifts are typical, yet no less traumatic and confusing for teenage boys. These extreme alterations in mood can happen repeatedly throughout the day, and often for no reason. One moment, a boy might feel very comfortable and self-assured; the next, he may plummet into a severe depression, or feel equally happy or even ecstatic for no apparent reason. Similarly, a friend might say a rude or negative comment, or a gesture from a girl may send the teen into an equally irrational mood.

Boys should be reminded that such mood shifts are a normal part of growing up. Once they are accepted as a natural expression of puberty, controlling them is then possible. In general, teens that are able to channel their energies into positive outlets, such as sporting events, social activities and schoolwork are better able to control their moods. Learning how to deal with anxiety and expectation are also very important.

☺☹ **Peer Pressure**

Human beings are social creatures, and the need for social acceptance is an important part of our design. Teens are especially dependent on their interaction with and opinions of others, particularly their own peers. Although such socialization is necessary and inevitable, it can also lead to problems of identity, self-image, and responsibility. Many teens are often confronted with an alarming double standard between what's considered acceptable to their friends and what's required from their parents and educators. Since the ongoing battle between guidance and independence will continue to rage throughout puberty and on into adulthood, open communication is very important.

When am I ready for sex?

♥ Infatuations

Every adult can remember his or her first "crush." Such teen infatuations can start as early as junior high school and continue well into college. As hormones begin to rage, eyes and hands can begin to wander. And what might have been ponytail pulling and chewing gum throwing in grade school has now blossomed into bona fide dating situations and even the opportunity for sexual intercourse.

The brew can be a potentially dangerous one; extreme mood shifts and sensitivity to peer pressure, coupled with seemingly overwhelming sexual desires and a marked lack of social and sexual experience can only lead to trouble without proper adult guidance and supervision.

Although sex education is a complex subject unto itself, everyone agrees that teens should be taught early on to differentiate a spontaneous "crush" from the reality of a life-long emotional and sexual commitment. Most high school sex education programs stress the need for abstinence as the smartest choice for minimizing the emotional pressures of adolescence, and, of course, the probability for unwanted pregnancies.

What can my parents do to make puberty easier for me?

ᛰ Adolescent First-Aid Packet

Complex problems often have fairly simple solutions. Although adolescence can be a particularly demanding time for both teens and their families, a few helpful suggestions might make the rough going a little smoother. Basic to all these suggestions is the importance of OPEN COMMUNICATION between teens and their families. Teens need love, and they need to be reminded that they are not alone. Most adolescent emotional problems can be helped and sometimes solved altogether through openness, honesty, and communication.

☑ Communicate!

No subject should be considered taboo. Teens should be encouraged to share what's on their mind. Of course, some adolescent behavior is perfectly acceptable, while others might not be. The only way teens can learn to differentiate between these many complex impulses and moods is if these subjects can be openly discussed and properly explained. After all, it's obviously much better to talk about uncomfortable or even potentially dangerous behaviors than to do them in secret and deal with the consequences later!

Therefore, an atmosphere where teens can feel comfortable when asking potentially embarrassing questions about their bodies and their minds should be promoted. By sharing their concerns, fears and feelings of disorientation and confusion, these feelings can actually be turned into expressions of family trust and encouragement. Simply by being given the chance to share experiences and feelings, teen isolation and vulnerability can be lessened or driven away completely. And by fostering such an open atmosphere, teens feel less of a need to carry around "secrets" or lie to their parents.

☑ Encouraging Self-Respect

The bottom line is self-respect. Teens lacking in self-respect are most likely to succumb to peer pressure, perform poorly in school, consume drugs and alcohol, or get involved in anti-social activities. Teen self-respect has much to do with how they are treated at home. Teens should be encouraged, yet also provided with a reasonable set of rules for acceptable and unacceptable forms of behavior. Whereas the details and even general approach to teaching teachers is well beyond the scope of this book, suffice to say that teen education begins and ends in the home.

Solitary Sexual Behavior

The old joke is that 90% of men and boys admit to masturbating—and the rest are liars! Let's take a peek at this often-misunderstood yet very important expression of human sexual function.

The word *masturbation* is derived from the Greek root "mezea" meaning "to arouse the genitals". Masturbation is a way in which sexual satisfaction and release is achieved through self-stimulation. Regardless of what most people hear or say, both men and women masturbate throughout their lives.

Does everyone masturbate?

Many boys feel some measure of guilt or shame about masturbation. Interestingly enough, there's a strong historical pattern, and most societies have viewed masturbation negatively. But contemporary psychologists and therapists all agree that masturbation is a natural expression of human sexuality.

Shared Sexual Behavior

Sex is a normal and inevitable part of adult human behavior and experience. Biologically, sex allows for the continuance of the species, and is, in this sense, perhaps the most basic and important human ability that exists. Emotionally, sex is also the most deep-rooted and potentially complex instinct.

Teenagers are caught in a tricky place: on the one hand, they are biologically fully "mature" in the sense that they are able to procreate; on the other, they lack the resources and experiences to have children in a way that is emotionally and socially acceptable.

When is the "right" time to have sex?

Adolescence is a challenging "waiting game," one where the body and the mind is able and very willing to participate in shared sexual behavior, while the family and society generally suggest that abstinence is probably the best policy. Indeed, unwanted pregnancies, the ever-present threat of STDs, and the emotional realities present in teen sex all suggest that sex education, in one form or another, is important and necessary.

Sex Education — For the Parents

Any way you look at it, sex education begins in the home. A parent's behavior influences and provides an example for his or her children. For example, whether or not (and to what extent) your own sex life is ever discussed, how you react to media images (what is considered acceptable or unacceptable), or even whether or not you kiss your spouse in public all have an effect on your children's view of sex and sexuality. Inevitably, your son will ask some questions: How you react to his questions can greatly influence his own attitude and approach to sex.

Although these situations can be awkward, one saying remains valid: "If you don't educate your children, someone else will." Information sources for your teen include friends, various media sources such as television and the movies, and even other adults. Of course, these sources can provide deceiving or incorrect information, or information that you, as a parent, don't agree with. Every child needs open communication, a strong set of values, good information and constant reinforcement of their self-worth. Who else can you trust to deliver such vital information?

Birth Control

The United States has the highest teen pregnancy rate in the industrialized world, even though teens in Germany, France and elsewhere seem to be having sex just as frequently. A big part of the problem is insufficient or inadequate sex education. Although many parents feel that the only practical approach to teen sexuality is abstinence, the fact remains that some teens are having sex. And not only are they having sex, but they are having unprotected sex, and sex without birth control.

If a teen does have sex, what's the best form of birth control and protection from STDs?

Put On Your Rubbers!

For men (and, if necessary, teenage boys), the most effective contraceptive device (and protector from sexually transmitted diseases) remains the latex condom. They are relatively inexpensive, readily available, and fairly easy to use.

Condom use alone has a failure rate of ten to twenty out of every 100 couples. This is why it is a good idea to use condoms along with other forms of birth control to increase their effectiveness. Most companies sell condoms that have already been coated with spermicide.

Once again, the only sure form of birth control and protection from STDs is abstinence. Similarly, many psychologists feel that teenagers are far too young to engage in sexual activity. But if teens engage in sexual activity, then they should be informed as to the proper method of birth control and protection.

Sexually Transmitted Diseases (STDs)

Whenever human bodies come into physical contact, the chance of sharing disease-causing organisms increases tremendously. Since sexual intercourse involves actual physical penetration, and often the sharing of bodily fluids, the risk of exposure to disease is particularly high.

A sexually transmitted disease, or "STD," is a disease caused by exactly this type of direct bodily contact. Since many different types of organisms and the diseases they cause can be transmitted from one person to the next, proper diagnosis and treatment can prove complicated. Similarly, these diseases affect different people differently, and a doctor should be consulted as soon as any one of a number of varied symptoms become apparent.

What are some of the symptoms of contracting an STD?

Although many of these symptoms can appear without the presence of an STD, they should be noted, and a doctor consulted:

- Discharge from the end of the penis
- Pain or burning when urinating
- Sores or blisters on the sex organs or in the mouth
- Swelling around the sex organs
- Running a temperature, experiencing chills

Can all STDs be cured?

Sadly, no. If detected early enough, some STDs, like gonorrhea, chlamydia and syphilis, can be completely cured with antibiotics. Viral STDs, such as genital herpes, hepatitis and HIV/AIDS cannot be cured, but their symptoms can be at least temporarily relieved.

In fact, these viral STDs are still present, and risk of infection is experienced with every sexual encounter. Teens should be made aware of these diseases, and how one reckless moment can, without the proper precautions, lead to a lifetime of illness and treatment. In fact, certain STDs can cause severe damage to the reproductive system, resulting in sterility. In other words, some of these diseases can destroy a teen's ability ever to father a child.

Can you describe some of these diseases?

Summary of STDs:

STD	What it is	Treatment
AIDS and HIV	⇨ Immune system is attacked, making the body more likely to get infections such as pneumonia.	⇨ Drug "cocktails" prevent the spread of the virus and kill blood cells already infected with it. ⇨ No cure

STD	What it is	Treatment
Chancroid	⇨ Bacterial "warts" in the mouth and around the genitals.	⇨ Antibiotics and skin "burning" agents.
Chlamydia	⇨ Bacterial infection of the genitals.	⇨ Antibiotics ⇨ Can cause permanent damage to sexual organs if left untreated.
Crabs	⇨ "Bugs" that nest in the pubic hair.	⇨ Various skin and hair treatment creams.
Herpes	⇨ Viral infection of the sex organs, anus or mouth. Leads to reddening irritation and bumps.	⇨ No cure ⇨ Medication can help treat symptoms.
Human Papilloma virus/Genital Warts	⇨ Virus that attacks the skin in exposed areas. ⇨ Warts results.	⇨ No cure ⇨ Medication can help control condition ⇨ Cauterization is sometimes performed.
Scabies	⇨ Skin disease that is caused by a parasite.	⇨ Treatable with antibiotics and skin creams.
Syphilis	⇨ Bacterial infection that can spread throughout the body.	⇨ Treatable with antibiotics.

How can STD's be prevented?

Prevention

Abstinence is the ONLY 100% sure way of avoiding these diseases. But if sexual activity occurs, latex condoms can give good protection because they are effective barriers (something that keeps two people's fluids from directly interacting). Again, using a condom isn't 100% safe against pregnancy or STD's—only abstinence is—but it offers the best protection from STD's available, and generally pretty good protection from pregnancy. Also, dental dams are available on the market as oral protection. A dental dam can be used in the mouth as a barrier to STD's during oral sex. Dental dams are available for both men and women to use.

Treatment

Different types of treatments are given for each STD. For some, treatment involves taking pills or getting a shot to kill the organism that caused the STD. Some STD's are viruses and cannot be cured, but treatment can ease the symptoms and stop more damage to the body. Treatments for viruses include pills, topical creams, freezing or burning of the infected area, or surgery.

Inspiration for the Boys

After your journey through this book, hopefully you are now clued in as to what is or will be happening to your body. Keep in mind that this book is designed to help explain what happens. When you are actually experiencing the physical, emotional, or psychological changes that were discussed, let your parents know what's going on. Being a teenager is hard enough. Having open discussions with your parents will help ease the tension that comes with puberty. Remember that your parents were once teenagers, too, and they will more than likely understand what you're going through and why these things are happening. Make smart choices and get to know yourself in all aspects before knowing a partner sexually.

978-0-595-37969-9
0-595-37969-9